Raising Happy Children

Using Numerology to Become a Better Parent

Joan L. Scibienski

Flint Hills Publishing

Raising Happy Children:
Using Numerology to Become a Better Parent
Copyright © 2021 Joan L. Scibienski
All rights reserved.

Cover Design by Amy Albright

Flint Hills Publishing
www.flinthillspublishing.com

Printed in the U.S.A.

ISBN: 978-1-953583-06-2

Library of Congress Application Pending

Table of Contents

Preface	1
1. What is Numerology?	3
2. How to Use Numerology	9
3. An Overview of What the Numbers Tell Us	21
4. The Birth Path Number	27
5. The Destiny/Expression Number	37
Computation Worksheets	45
6. How Do I Apply These Numbers to My Child?	53
7. If Your Child Has a Master Number	83
8. Karmic Challenge Numbers	89
9. Putting It All Together	95
Just For Fun Practice Charts	115
Conclusion	123
References	125
About the Author	127

Preface

The goal of most parents is to raise healthy, happy children. But, as every parent knows, no two children are alike. Even twins can have vastly different personalities. Some children are loving and gentle while others are always moving, never wanting to stay in one place for very long. Some excel at school, exhibiting excellent memories and the ability to work hard toward their goals, while others bore easily and rebel against any form of authority. Sibling's personalities can vary significantly in a family. Despite having the same parents, gene pool, and environment for their upbringing, children may still exhibit very different characteristics and behaviors.

In my long career as a psychic intuitive, I have found a way to help parents understand the reasons for the seemingly inexplicable differences they often find in their own children. Through the ancient science of numerology, I will describe how the birth date and birth name can make a vast difference in a child's behavior. I will teach you how to take this information and use it in different computations. From these results, you will be able to apply my recommendations for parenting techniques based on the information you uncover. You will learn effective approaches to deal with a particular child's personality, and understand their potentials for both positive and negative behaviors.

Having a more complete understanding of our children and their unique personalities can make us more effective parents. Our children need and deserve this. After all, they are a precious, and at times, most challenging gift from the Universe!

CHAPTER 1

What is Numerology?

Numerology is the study of numbers. It is an ancient "occult science" that originated from the Jewish book of mysticism, the *Kabbalah*, and was introduced to Western civilization by the Greek mathematician Pythagoras (569-470 B.C.). It is based on the concept that our world is energy and all energy holds a charge or vibration, including numbers. By learning and applying some relatively simple information, you can discover certain aptitudes and character traits of yourself or others. Much like decoding a secret message, a person's date of birth and name can be used to uncover information about that person. These numbers create potentials in life, both positive and negative. A person's numbers can help describe character traits, talents, stumbling blocks, life lessons, life purpose, and even motivations.

If you are new to the idea that there is information available to us that comes from places beyond our physical senses, welcome to the exciting ideas and practices from those of us who are obsessed with all things "metaphysical." My metaphysical journey is a long and complex one. The short version of my story is that when I was seven years old, I was in a fever-induced coma for several days. During that time, I met my spirit guides, what many call angels. When I woke from the coma, completely healthy, I soon discovered I could communicate with entities on the Other Side. As an adult I have had several careers. I've been a nurse, an EMT, a drug and alcohol counselor, a realtor. In my 30s, it became clear to me that my true calling was to be a full-time intuitive counselor, a psychic that counsels people in an effort to help them live the life they were meant to live. In my sessions with clients, I receive information from a variety of sources: contact with their spirit guides, their deceased loved ones, accessing the Akashic Records (a great topic to research for those of you just learning about metaphysics), putting together astrological charts, and last, but certainly not least, numerology.

Numerology is perhaps the easiest life map to understand and learn. It's different from astrology in that you don't need complex books or a computer program. All you need are the person's birth date and their complete name as it appears on their birth certificate, a piece of paper, and a writing implement.

Many of you may be wondering how it is possible that information can be generated from sources that you might think are random. We just happen to be born on a day hopefully close to a nine-month gestation after our inception, right? And our parents, maybe with the help of others, have selected our names, right? But what if these assumptions are not accurate? Students of metaphysics have a different view of our birthdays and our given names.

Like other metaphysical tools, numerology starts with the fundamental idea that there is existence beyond our physical senses: that consciousness survives death. And though the understanding of "what is God" is far beyond this discussion, for purposes of explaining something like numerology, it is important to recognize the source of the information does come from a loving force, regardless of the name you might want to attach to it. In numerology, the numbers and the explanations attached to them are not random. It is difficult to know the original source of the information. It seems reasonable to state that many Jews feel the *Kabbalah* was channeled from God. Pythagoras purportedly learned about numerology from one of the "mystery schools"—institutions that can be traced back 3,500 years ago that had goals of serving God and keeping ancient knowledge alive. From my own personal experience, I have worked with thousands of clients and have seen firsthand how patterns emerge from numbers. I have also received information psychically which confirms to me what I have been taught and learned on my own regarding the subject of numerology. And as a mother of a very tenacious son who is now a wonderful father, I can assure you that having an understanding of numerology gave me extremely helpful insight in parenting my own child.

Even if all of this stuff about consciousness and mystery schools sounds bizarre to you, I challenge you to delve into the information about numerology. Once you have the basics down, practice what you've learned by doing the numerology of family members or famous people and compare what you know about their lives to what is revealed by their numbers. Taking the time to do some numerology practice will help you achieve the purpose of this book: to teach you to compute and understand the numerology of your own child with the goal of helping you better parent your unique child. At the very least, you will gain more information that will help you understand your child's personality. Hopefully this understanding will give insight that will make you a more patient and effective parent.

I do need to provide an important caveat; this book is by no means a full education on the science and practice of numerology. In fact, it is a very general treatise on how to apply the numbers and what they mean. If you went to a professional numerologist (and yes, there are many reputable ones working in this field), the information they would provide for you would be much more in-depth than what I will cover in this book. It should, however, be an easy-to-use primer to help you with your child.

CHAPTER 2

How to Use Numerology

It is important to understand that even though numerology is about numbers, the math to determine those numbers is quite easy. A precocious six year old could probably do the calculations required in numerology. All you need to do is add together numbers until you arrive at a single digit.

For example: 3 + 9 = 12.

Then reduce that to 1 + 2 = 3.

It's that easy.

The first step in analyzing a person's numerology is to put together a "numerology chart." There are thirteen numbers used in constructing the chart. These numbers are 1, 2, 3, 4, 5, 6, 7, 8, 9, 11, 22, 33, and 44. To determine what numbers exist in a particular person's chart requires adding together the numbers of the birth date and the corresponding numbers of the letters of the full birth name. **Remember:** you are working to achieve a single digit, so always reduce the larger numbers until they appear as a single digit. This is accomplished by continuing to add together the number until it is a single digit.

For example: 1949 would look like—
$1 + 9 + 4 + 9 = 23 = 2 + 3 = 5$.

Each of these numbers represents different characteristics and ways of expressing those characteristics which will be explained shortly.

Every number that shows up in your chart has significance. Yet there are some numbers that have more significance than others. You may have numbers in your chart that are called "Master Numbers." The meanings behind these numbers are more powerful and can hint at challenges your Soul has provided to you. Think of these challenges as opportunities for growth! You will know you have uncovered a Master Number if the individual numbers when added result in an **11, 22, 33, or 44**. This is the only exception to the rule of reducing the larger numbers down to a single digit; **don't reduce these numbers.** They are reputedly intensified versions of the single digit numbers they replace: 2, 4, 6, and 8. When a person has these numbers in their charts, the Soul is requiring more of the person. Often that person feels compelled toward an achievement that benefits more than themselves. In general, people with Master Numbers seem to have a potential for a high degree of learning and achievement. Many people find it hard to live up to the goals outlined by their Master Number potential and will instead use the number in its lowest vibrational octave. To put it simply, their Soul may want the person living on Earth to reach for the stars, but instead, the person decides it's just too darn hard. Lucky me, my kid has a bunch of Master Numbers!

Before we get into the specifics about how to calculate the numbers, it is important to understand there are five different calculations that I use in obtaining information. These calculations result in **five core numbers** which represent different facets of a person's life. One of the most important of these five numbers I call the **"Birth Path."** (If you look at other sources of information about numerology, you may see the term "Life Path." This is just a different name for the same concept.) This number represents what you are here to do. It reveals your most fulfilling direction and the major lessons you are here to learn. It gives a broad outline of the opportunities and challenges you will encounter and the personal traits that you can utilize to reach a positive conclusion of your journey. The positive aspects of the Birth Path number show the skills and abilities you possess, while the negative aspects of the number are traits you must learn to balance.

The second most relevant number in a chart is the **"Destiny Number."** (It is also called the "Expression Number.") It reveals your talents and abilities as well as many of your natural interests. It can show you the kind of career you will excel in and the opportunities and talents you have at your disposal.

As I mentioned before, this book is not designed to be a comprehensive treatise on numerology. There are, however, three additional calculations that are important. These numbers represent different facets of your personality. The **"Heart's Desire Number"** (sometimes labeled the "Soul Urge") reveals your desires at the very deepest level. Ultimately, it explains the reason for many of your actions. It is what you crave deep within your Soul that often is unseen by others. The **"Personality Number"** (sometimes called the "Outer Number") is the face you show the world: your personality traits, how you dress and act in public. Your **"Day Number"** reveals your approach to reaching you Birth Path and, I believe, reveals how you see yourself.

Using Theodor Seuss Geisel as an Example to Calculate Numerology:
Dr. Seuss's Birth Path:

The best way to understand how to determine numerology is through the use of examples. Let's analyze the numerology of one of our greatest children's authors, Dr. Seuss. He was born on 3-2-1904. To figure out Dr. Seuss's Birth Path, add together all the numbers, then reduce them to a single digit: $3 + 2 + 1 + 9 + 0 + 4 = 19/10/1$ which is reduced as $1 + 9 = 10 = 1 + 0 = 1$. We now know that Dr. Seuss's Birth Path Number is 1. (I will explain the meaning of the numbers in the next chapter, for now we are just learning how to do the calculations.)

Mathematically, there are two possible equations that can reach the number 1: $1 + 0$ or $1 +$

9. Some numerologists, myself included, believe it is beneficial to understand how the 1 was derived in order to get a clear picture of "what type of 1" we are dealing with. We know from this example that Seuss is a 19/1. We can look to the meanings behind the individual numbers 1 and 9 to get more information about the characteristics of this particular number 1: Seuss must be original (a characteristic of the number 1) while still acting for the benefit of humanity (a quality of the number 9) in order to effectively live an independent life (the goal of the number 1). On the other hand, if his 1 were reached by the numbers 1 and 0, he would be concerned with using his own abilities solely (an attribute of the number 1) without considering the needs of the greater good.

To determine the remaining facets requires us to convert Seuss's full birth name from letters to numbers. Each letter of the alphabet is represented by a number, one through nine. The following table provides the conversion:

1	2	3	4	5	6	7	8	9
A	B	C	D	E	F	G	H	I
J	K	L	M	N	O	P	Q	R
S	T	U	V	W	X	Y	Z	

Seuss's Destiny Number:

In doing the conversion from letters to numbers, always consider the full birth name as it appears on the birth certificate, even if it was misspelled or the person was later adopted and given a new legal name. Any later change in name for any reason is not relevant; if a person changed their name after they married, the married name is not considered relevant. The only name that matters for purposes of numerology is the full name as it appears on the person's birth certificate without using any name suffixes like Jr., Senior, or 2nd. In Dr. Seuss's case, his birth name was Theodor Seuss Geisel. Using the letter-to-number conversion table, we can convert Dr. Seuss's full name to a number representation and then simply add all the numbers together:

$$2+8+5+6+4+6+9+1+3+5+1+1+7+5+9+1+5+3$$
$$=81$$

Then reduce as $8 + 1 = 9$.

Thus, Seuss's Destiny Number is 9.

Seuss's Heart's Desire Number:

The Heart's Desire Number is found by adding together all the vowels in the name until a single digit is found. The letter Y is considered a vowel if there is no vowel next to it and it is being used to represent a vowel. Admittedly, this can be much more difficult to ascertain with some spellings of foreign names.

Again, using the results we obtained from the letter-to-number conversion table, we find that "Theodor" has three vowels: the letter "e" which is represented by the number 5, and two "o's" represented by the number 6. "Seuss" has two vowels: an "e" which is represented by the number 5, and the "u" which is represented by the number 3. And finally, Geisel has three vowels: two "e's" represented by the number 5, and an "i" represented by the number 9. We therefore calculate one of America's most celebrated children's author's Heart's Desire as:

$$5 + 6 + 6 = 17 \text{ for the first name,}$$
$$\text{and } 5 + 3 = 8 \text{ for the middle name,}$$
$$\text{and } 5 + 9 + 5 = 19.$$

Then we add them together: $17 + 8 + 19 = 44/8$ which is a Master Number and never reduced.

Dr. Seuss's Heart's Desire Number is 44/8.

Seuss's Personality Number:

The Personality Number is based on the consonants in a name. As mentioned earlier, it has more to do with how others see you; it represents your outer personality.

To obtain Dr. Seuss's Personality Number, we add the numbers from the consonants for his first name:

$$2 + 8 + 4 + 9 = 23,$$
$$\text{and his middle name: } 1 + 1 + 1 = 3,$$
$$\text{and his last name: } 7 + 1 + 3 = 11.$$

Add these together: 23 + 3 + 11 = 37.
Reduce by adding 3 + 7= 10 = 1 + 0 = 1
for a *Personality Number of 1.*

Seuss's Day Number:

This final core number is the easiest to calculate. It is quite simply the day of birth. Therefore, *Dr. Seuss's day number is 2*. As you will learn later, in general the number 2 means added intuition, good humor, and a cooperative nature.

Math class is over! That's all the calculating you need to do in order to know how to derive the numbers associated with a particular person. Now the fun starts—learning what the numbers mean.

CHAPTER 3

An Overview of What the Numbers Tell Us

Now that you know how the numbers are derived, it's time to understand the meaning of the numbers. It must be understood that numbers have both positive and negative vibrations and a person can fluctuate to either extreme or be consistent. As humans, we will rarely act only at our highest and best. We often act out the negative patterns of the numbers, too. If there is a Master Number to consider, the traits associated with that particular number, either positive or negative, will be more emphasized in that person.

Here are keywords for each number. A more thorough description will come when describing how the numbers work as Birth Path and Destiny numbers.

Key Words Descriptor:

Positive traits: individuality, self-starters, independent, original.

Negative traits: selfish, dependent, lazy, egotistical, self-absorbed, narcissist.

Positive traits: cooperative, good partners, balanced, mediator, peacemaker.

Negative traits: stubborn, codependent, worrier, indecisive, apathetic.

Positive traits: creative, communicative, peaceful, harmonious, effervescent.

Negative traits: moody, withdrawn, spoiled, superficial, frivolous, intolerant, manipulative.

Positive traits: planner, fixer, builder, practical, dependable, loyal.

Negative traits: stubborn, rigid, narrow-minded, oppressive, potential for violence.

Positive traits: exuberant, exciting, progressive, free spirit, great communicator.

Negative traits: lack of direction, sociopathic, irresponsible, sensualist, liar, manipulator.

Positive traits: nurturing, honest, responsible, idealistic, humanitarian, helpful, loyal.

Negative traits: martyr, depressive, critical, exaggeration, meddling, guilt.

Positive traits: analytical, observant, spiritual, hard worker, very caring.

Negative traits: pessimistic, dreamer, terrible with money, loner, sarcastic.

Positive traits: leadership, organized, ambitious, money creator, hard worker.

Negative traits: oppressive, bombastic, arrogant, obsessed with accumulating money and status, unemotional.

Positive traits: compassionate, idealistic, spiritual, humanitarian, non-prejudice.

Negative traits: easily depressed, worrier, escapist, dreamer, overly sensitive, addictive personality.

CHAPTER 4

The Birth Path Number

The Birth Path number is of utmost importance in a person's numerology chart. This number can reveal our strongest-held values and predict future challenges. As mentioned earlier, this is the number that will be most revealing when it comes to giving you a broad understanding of opportunities you will have in your life as well as the challenges and lessons your Soul intends for you to learn. The following explanations of the individual numbers are to provide a deeper explanation of what a particular number means in the context of understanding your Birth Path.

Personal Mission: To develop creatively and confidently through independence, boldness, and innovation, as well as finding your own individual identity. Learning to depend on yourself you must overcome loneliness in order to find your own voice and your own way.

Life Purpose: To bring positive creative energy into the world through your natural leadership qualities and individuality.

Skills: Ingenuity, individuality, self-starter, independent, leadership.

Possible Negative Traits: To think that your way is the only way and not heed the advice of others. Egomania.

Personal Mission: To develop cooperation and balance without losing self. Learning to work in and for groups while keeping the spirit of cooperation in the forefront. Helping to bring divergent forces together for the good of all.

Life Purpose: Learn to work with others for higher goals, harmony, and mutual respect.

Skills: Diplomatic, an arbitrator, master of tact and persuasion, sincere, builder of consensus.

Possible Negative Traits: Codependency and inability to act effectively if challenged, shyness, and lack of courage causing failure to take action. Fear of moving forward without complete consensus so that you give up without even trying.

Personal Mission: To develop creative expression and sensitivity and recognize your ability to understand people.

Life Purpose: To use your wonderful sensitivity and creativity to uplift and heal.

Skills: Gifted in the use of speech and written communication, inspired thinking, visionary plans, accurate insights, a positive and inspirational spirit. Very creative with a gift for color, style, and decoration.

Possible Negative Traits: Manipulative, emotionally sensitive, not assertive, extravagant, lack of direction, moodiness, overly critical, unforgiving, lazy and entitled.

Birth Path Number 4

Personal Mission: To develop stability and structure, security, and a step-by-step process in all aspects of life in order to meet goals.

Life Purpose: Make goals and plan a step-by-step process for attaining security and stability. Being the foundation for completion, you are the rock for maintaining structure and seeing that goals are completed.

Skills: Excellent management skills, commonsensical, scientific approach, work to achieve goals and overcome obstacles, determined, careful planner, attention to detail.

Possible negative traits: Stubborn and fixed, argumentative, slow to change when change is needed, caught up in detail, slow to make decisions or change, need to control and regulate in an effort to put things in order. Possibly easily frustrated and frustration may lead to violent action.

Personal mission: To find freedom and learn discipline. To learn a little about everything. To live a full, active life.

Life purpose: Your life purpose is to find inner freedom through discipline, focus, and depth of experience.

Skills: Enthusiasm and zest for life. Fearlessness, progressive ideas, inventive, resourceful, fights for freedom, independent, quick thinker, energetic, inquisitive, and carefree.

Possible negative traits: Sociopathy, rationalization, restlessness, inability to commit, sensualist, risk-taker, liar, bores easily, never completes a task, undependable.

Personal Mission: To develop vision, acceptance, nurturing, championing justice always working with a deep sense of responsibility and caring.

Life Purpose: To reconcile your high ideals with practical reality and to accept yourself, the world, and the present moment by accepting the world as it is, not as you desire it to be. To help others and be a champion for the common good.

Skills: Compassion, empathy, nurturing, idealistic humanitarian, committed, and accepting of responsibility.

Potential Negative Traits: Stubbornness, obstinacy, self-righteousness, dominating posture, easily victimized, pessimistic, complainer, judgmental, martyr.

Birth Path Number 7

Personal Mission: To develop and accept your sense of spirituality, intuition, trust, and openness. To develop your scientific skills and also to learn to accept the world as it is, not for how you think it should be.

Life Purpose: To develop your sense of higher purpose, trust yourself and others, and trust in the process of your life so that you can feel safe enough to open up and share your wisdom and ideas with the world.

Skills: Brilliance, spirituality, inventive, researcher, investigation, circumspection, foresight, analysis, scientific, thinking, penetrating wit and acumen.

Possible Negative Traits: Dreamer, unrealistic, isolates, overly reserved and secretive, shrewdness, bossy, sarcastic, cynical, over-analyzing, argumentative, harsh temperament, conviction to a fault, never feeling like part of the world.

Personal Mission: Shrewd handling of resources in order to develop abundance, power, and the satisfaction that comes from success in the material world.

Life Purpose: To use your power and financial resources in order to help our world and other people.

Skills: Leader, executive abilities, political skills, expert handling of power and authority, master of gaining recognition and respect, sound judgment, organization, hardworking, decisive and commanding.

Possible Negative Traits: Lacks true humanitarian feelings, lack of empathy, impatient, overly ambitious and critical, repressing others, dogmatic, over reaching, expresses anger, love of display, argumentative, and dominating.

Personal Mission: To develop one's spirituality, creativity, philanthropy, integrity and wisdom.

Life Purpose: To live your life with integrity and in line with your heart's intuitive wisdom, always giving generously, and inspiring others by your good example.

Skills: Compassionate, idealistic, concern for mankind, highly spiritual, lives by philanthropic principles, dramatic thinking.

Possible Negative Traits: Moody and depressive with a tendency toward addiction, impulsive, changeable behavior, scattered energies, too much desire for personal recognition, terrible self-image, possible suicidal tendencies.

CHAPTER 5

The Destiny/Expression Number

The second most important number that bears consideration is the Destiny/Expression Number. While the Birth Path number explains what you have come to learn and your primary purpose in this lifetime, your Destiny/Expression Number describes the manner you will go about achieving this purpose. We have to take time and effort to achieve our Birth Path; the Destiny Number shows us the road we will travel and techniques we need to help us get there.

The Destiny/Expression Number can reveal a lot about your life purpose. It shows you your opportunities for success and your stumbling blocks to achieving that success. For instance, if you have a 6 Destiny Number, your opportunities for success will always include responsibility and humanitarianism. Whereas a Number 5 Destiny will achieve through experiencing as much of life as possible, taking risks and expressing their uniqueness. The Destiny Number is how you are destined to achieve and express your life purpose. It can offer ideas to you about how you can make the most out of your life experiences. It can help you pick a career that will be the best fit for you and benefit you the most at fulfilling your life path.

Destiny Number 1

Number 1: Your destiny demands that you be independent. You are here to express your own individuality, to achieve and initiate, and be a leader. Watch out for arrogance, self-doubt, and narcissism.

Number 2: Your destiny demands that you mediate, cooperate, harmonize, adapt, focus on a higher good, and socialize in such a way as to become the peacemaker. Watch out for pessimism, depression, codependency, indecisive, or passive-aggressive tendencies.

Number 3: Your destiny demands that you use your wonderful sensitivity and creativity to uplift and heal. Watch out for wasteful activity, indecisiveness, manipulation, emotional ups and downs, depression, or being judgmental, critical, and having the tendency to over-think everything or to become lazy.

Destiny Number 4

Number 4: Your destiny demands that you build something of lasting value through your hard work and stable and secure outlook. Guard against stubbornness, obstinacy, self-righteousness, dominating posture, easily becoming a victim, pessimism, complaining, and being judgmental.

Destiny Number 5

Number 5: Your destiny demands that you affect change and show people how to live joyous, free lives. Embrace your fearlessness and taste all life has to offer, and then communicate what you've learned. Watch out for sociopathy, selfishness, not being able to keep commitments, hedonism, hurting others, self-absorption, and chaos. Learn to understand and accept some boundaries.

Destiny Number 6

Number 6: Your destiny demands that you nurture and serve, love unconditionally, balance and modulate your sense of responsibility, and integrate your highly intuitive abilities with your down-to-earth, responsible nature. Watch out for martyrdom, disillusionment, taking on everyone else's problems, self-righteousness, codependency, and being judgmental.

Destiny Number 7

Number 7: Your destiny demands that you find your own answer for the meaning of life. Spiritual and inventive, you nonetheless are excellent at analyzing. You are also quite intuitive and must learn to blend these two different parts of your consciousness. You must share your hard-won wisdom with the world. Watch out for cynicism, withdrawal, disillusionment, depression, sarcasm, not being able to sustain loving relationships, idealism not based in fact, and irresponsibility, especially with money. Learn to live in this world, not the one you wish for.

Destiny Number 8

Number 8: Your destiny demands leadership, executive abilities, political skills, expert handling of power and authority, mastering how to gain recognition and respect, sound judgment, organization, hard work, and the abilities to be decisive and commanding. Possible negative traits include: lacking true humanitarian feelings, empathy, patience. The 8 Destiny can be overly ambitious and critical, repress others, be dogmatic, over reaching, and angry. They can have a love of display, be argumentative and dominating, ruthless, overbearing, and stubborn. They may give up when the road gets rough or push intimate relationships away.

Destiny Number 9

Number 9: Your destiny demands that you understand higher consciousness and help others achieve this knowledge. Yours is a spiritual path and you're here to love unconditionally, as a humanitarian. Someone with a 9 Destiny is on a profound journey that offers opportunities to touch the lives of others and heal deep wounds. A person with a 9 Destiny is learning how to both give and receive. They may find that they must give up many worldly things, including some relationships, but as they are old Souls, they understand how to proceed with going forward, even through loss. They must watch out for disillusionment, rationalization, becoming delusional, righteous, being gullible or intolerant. They can be easily hurt then not release the hurt. There can be a tendency toward depression and resentment.

Computations

Name: _____

Date of Birth: _____

Birth Path Number:

Destiny/Expression Number:

Heart's Desire Number:

Personality Number:

Day Number:

Computations

Name: _____

Date of Birth: _____

Birth Path Number:

Destiny/Expression Number:

Heart's Desire Number:

Personality Number:

Day Number:

Computations

Name: _____

Date of Birth: _____

Birth Path Number:

Destiny/Expression Number:

Heart's Desire Number:

Personality Number:

Day Number:

Computations

Name: _____

Date of Birth: _____

Birth Path Number:

Destiny/Expression Number:

Heart's Desire Number:

Personality Number:

Day Number:

Computations

Name: _____

Date of Birth: _____

Birth Path Number:

Destiny/Expression Number:

Heart's Desire Number:

Personality Number:

Day Number:

Computations

Name: _____

Date of Birth: _____

Birth Path Number:

Destiny/Expression Number:

Heart's Desire Number:

Personality Number:

Day Number:

Computations

Name: _____

Date of Birth: _____

Birth Path Number:

Destiny/Expression Number:

Heart's Desire Number:

Personality Number:

Day Number:

Computations

Name: _____

Date of Birth: _____

Birth Path Number:

Destiny/Expression Number:

Heart's Desire Number:

Personality Number:

Day Number:

CHAPTER 6

How Do I Apply These Numbers to My Child?

Now that you have computed the numbers for your child, and you have the results for each category we've discussed, use the information in this chapter as an answer key for getting information about your child, keeping in mind that the true person is not ascertained by only one of the numbers, but by the combination of numbers. This can be a bit more difficult if the child has a combination of both odd and even numbers. Odd numbers are more introverted and rely more on themselves, while even numbers are people-oriented and need others to utilize their numbers fully. If the child has an even distribution, they may vacillate between the two opposites. If the numbers are split less evenly, look to the position of the number to see in which area they will be initiator or the follower.

Number 1 Birth Path

As you can tell from the description of the numbers, a child with a 1 Birth Path will be a very different child from one with a 2 Birth Path. While the 2 will usually be gentle and accommodating, wanting to be pals and have lots of friends, the 1 will thrive when allowed to be a leader. He needs to feel that he is independent and that he can have original ideas and proceed unencumbered to actualize those ideas. Schooling should involve independent thinking and the child should feel as though she is not being controlled. They are leaders, and often object to being led. Thus, they do not always play well with others. Success in school will have more to do with interest and attention than an actual desire to learn. They must have the correct guidance from adults otherwise the 1 could become selfish, bullheaded, and pushy; there is the potential he or she could become the class bully. The 1 is the epitome of a first or only child.

When the 1 is the Birth Day number the tendency for independence is pronounced, especially in childhood. They will often do their best if allowed to work alone; they need ample freedom to fully develop and express their unique creativity and leadership. As children, there will be times they appear aloof and detached. This is the 1 Birth Day child attempting to develop their inner independence. If a child with this number needs to be punished, discuss why, then work with them to come up with an appropriate punishment. If they will not work with you, then offer them five potential punishments; let them pick which one they think they can accept. As a parent of a child with this number, it is important to remember that having their independence restricted will be very hard on the child unless the child has a clear picture as to why they are being punished and for how long. You want them to understand that you are not just asserting your authority, but are working with them so that they will find a way to exist in our world of rules without always feeling controlled.

When the 1 appears as the Destiny Number it adds initiative and independence to whatever the Birth Path Number is. For example, if the Birth Path is the 2, the child's work with others will be more creative and inventive.

An important caveat about the Number 1 personality is that often females will be afraid to use this number correctly. Many girls are raised to think they should be gentle and cooperative, the opposite of the 1, which can cause them to become "the woman behind the man," rather than exhibiting her powers of leadership and independence.

Possible career choices for the Number 1:
As stated in the description, this number produces leaders and initiators. Consequently,

children with the Number 1 Birth Path are meant to be their own bosses, not to be subordinate to anyone. They have the potential to become good business owners, doctors, government officials—any career that requires independence, creativity, and leadership.

Number 2 Birth Path

This number creates a gentle, sensitive, supportive, and possibly timid child. This child may be your cuddler, and is much more a follower than an initiator. These children love to be directed. They are also loyal and very supportive. Because of their need to be bonded to others, these children can be quite intuitive and can sense when others are unhappy. This can cause them to work to create peace at all costs. They can merge their egos with others, but this tendency can also cause them to become too needy or co-dependent. They can become quite insecure, self-effacing, and shy if these tendencies are not addressed early. As long as they are not rejected by other school children, but instead feel as though they belong, they can do well in school. It will be important that they like their teachers and that their teachers like them. When these children need punishment, it is important to understand that they can be very hard on themselves. Therefore, when their behavior warrants a punishment, make sure it is explained that they are loved even though they are receiving a punishment; they are not bad, only the behavior is. Effective strategies for punishment of these children include assigning extra chores or not being able to attend a favored event or social situation. If the child is especially sensitive, it may be enough to explain what they did wrong and how it made you feel: disappointed, sad, unhappy, for example. Because they have such deep empathy and a strong need to be liked, understanding cause and effect through how their actions were received by those involved can help them to change the behavior.

When the 2 is the Birth Day Number it increases the child's intuitive nature. Because of their natural empathetic abilities, these children, when they are working closely with someone, need to work with people who have a bright, happy disposition, otherwise they will adapt their behaviors to those they are around and become easily depressed or insecure. These children are reliable, trustworthy, and supportive. They don't necessarily seek the limelight, but enjoy helping those that do. They need praise and respond best to positive reinforcement rather than punishment.

When the 2 appears as the Destiny Number it adds cooperation, support, loyalty, and sensitivity to the Birth Path Number. For example, if the Birth Path Number is 1, a 2 Destiny Number would pare down the potential egotism or ruthlessness that could develop and help make the 1 more capable of working well with others.

Possible career choices for the Number 2:
Number 2 people are very creative, knowledge-oriented, smart, charming, and soft spoken. These

qualities may lead them into positions of negotiation, mediation, ambassador, diplomat, public relations officer, consultant, matchmaker, sales person, or teacher. Cooperation is the theme for the Number 2 Birth Path. They work well with others, but are not always self-starters. Because they can work well within groups and can help others see both sides of any issue, this trait can help in some areas of the law and arbitration or meditation. The Number 2 has natural healing abilities and may find work in alternative medicine, massage, and nursing. If a Number 2 can control his or her sensitivity, they do well as counselors.

Number 3 Birth Path

This is the number of the expressive, creative child. Number 3 children are enthusiastic, joyous, charming, helpful, and friendly. They have a natural gift of expressing themselves and like entertaining others. They thrive within a mellow, gentle, fun-loving family. They will try to avoid confrontation and strife. When hurt or surrounded by negativity, they often withdraw. Taken to an extreme, there is the potential they can live in a world of their own creation. The Number 3 Birth Path child is generally optimistic, generous, and enjoys the finer things of life. They are social and like to be the life of the party. Sometimes their need to be liked can lead to manipulation and superficiality. They must be guided to learn discipline and commitment. Teach them early to make decisions and deal with consequences. Make sure they are taught the value of money or they will be quite extravagant and irresponsible. If school for these children involves a lot of socializing and feeling as though they belong and are liked, they will do well. However, because these children have the potential to occasionally become lazy, parents need to be aware of the need to enforce good study habits. Regarding punishment, parents must remember that this child has a very sensitive disposition; it is good to explain to them that you are punishing the behavior and that you still love them. They will respond best by having something they like taken away for a period of time or by restricting an activity, especially social media.

When the 3 is the Birth Day they are fun-loving extroverts and can be quite the entertainers. However, occasionally the 3 Birth Day can have a critical nature that they must learn to curb.

When the 3 appears as the Destiny Number their creativity and sensitivity will help them to be uplifting to other people.

Possible career choices for the Number 3: Creativity is the mainstay children for the Number 3 Birth Path. They have a natural sense of style and balance and make excellent designers, actors, musicians, and writers. They can also do well as party or wedding planners because they are social and keep up with many of the trends. They can be a great inspiration to others because of their natural pleasant, uplifting natures. Social media influencer, web designers, media in general, could also be good positions for them.

Number 4 Birth Path

This is the number of security and stability. These children need structure and order. They are down-to-earth, strong-willed, with firm ideas about right and wrong. They are precise and tenacious and can appear quite stubborn and fixed. They need orderly ways to vent their frustration because they can become bossy, vengeful, or on rare occasions, violent. With clear direction and guidance, these children are dependable and hard working. They are very loyal and like responsibility. They can work independently, as long as they have a clear idea of what is needed, but they are also great team players. Many of these children can do well in school as long as everything is explained thoroughly. They are not particularly fast learners but, if things are spelled out, or they can actually have more hands-on learning, they will do much better. It is a good educational strategy for these children to write out instructions they can follow. When you are working with them, write out each task and then give them a star or a check mark when these are completed.

When they receive a certain number of stars or check marks, they receive something of their choosing. Do not think these children are "slow." They may appear that way, but they are not; they are methodical. If they are not taught to share and have deep values, they can become quite materialistic as they age. They will thrive if they are taught a step-by-step approach to all things. Teach them cause-and-effect early. Taking this approach with them helps them feel secure and stable. A good way to begin may be through planting a garden. Through that procedure they will see how planting a seed, watering the seed, and keeping weeds down, will produce a positive outcome such as a favorite vegetable or a beautiful flower. When punishment is needed, explain why, then choose something that does not make the child feel insecure: extra chores or being grounded, for example. Just always be consistent. Don't back down on the punishment once employed and make sure the punishment fits the "crime."

When the 4 is the Birth Day Number they are practical and good with their hands. However, this can increase the potential for the child to become materialistic. Teach them to share.

When the 4 appears as the Destiny Number it creates a methodical, organized, and systematic approach to life. They will bring structure, dependability, and management skills to wherever they are needed.

Possible career choices for the Number 4: Number 4 people are critical thinkers and multi-talented individuals. These people will make money through hard work. The Number 4 Birth Path children are likely to become builders, actuaries, accountants, editors, technologists, bankers, or engineers. They like anything that comes together systematically, logically, and practically. They like direction and follow orders well. They are precise, tenacious, and exacting. They make excellent business professionals as well as mechanics, construction workers, farmers, and landscape professionals.

Number 5 Birth Path

This is the number of freedom, adventure, and learning through multiple experiences. These children are quite active and learn best by doing, rather than sitting quietly. They love meeting people and are very social in groups. This, too, can create problems in their schooling as they like to talk and can become the "class clown." They are generally happy-go-lucky children as long as they are not restricted or held back from doing what they want to do or have an overly structured routine. When that happens, they can become manipulative, contrary—or at the very worst extreme—sociopathic. This is the luckiest of all numbers as 5s seem to come out of most situations smelling like a rose. These children are multi-talented and very diverse in their abilities and interests, but can lose interest rapidly and leave many projects unfinished. Many are quite good at sports and need to be physical in order to burn-off excess energy.

When it comes to punishments, the parent must teach these children very early to accept the parent's authority. Punishments must be discussed including an explanation as to what type of behavior is considered punishable. There must be a consensus between the adult and the child on this point, otherwise the child will not allow themselves to be punished. These are the children that when told to stay in a particular spot will simply walk away and begin to play somewhere else, or when they are teenagers, will ignore being grounded and instead escape through their bedroom windows. If this child is punished by the assignment of extra chores, they will most likely be done haphazardly. When they are older and are punished by the removal of possessions, this child will strive to replace them, even if they need to steal to do so. As you can see, punishing a 5 can prove difficult. Do not resort to corporal punishment out of frustration as this will only make them worse. This is why it is essential that they understand your authority early and acquiesce to it. Work on coming to a mutual consensus, and given these tendencies, perhaps use bribery instead of punishment.

When the 5 is the birth day the child needs variety, adventure, and excitement. They are highly adaptable, but can also be irresponsible, always looking to the next new thing. The parent must teach discipline. A 5 in any position can create a propensity for overindulgence in drugs, alcohol, food, sex—anything that heightens pleasure.

When the 5 appears as the Destiny Number it adds gaiety, freedom, fun, and excitement. The 5 is multitalented and is at ease with everybody, so a 5 Destiny adds the ability to work well with others—even those from different nationalities and cultures—and creates limitless possibilities in life.

Possible careers choices for the Number 5: Variety and change are what the Number 5 Birth Path needs and they can find success in a variety of fields. As long as what they do is stimulating to them, they can do it. They do not do well in routine jobs and will either be scattered in their work or change jobs often. Journalism, tour guide, sales, promotion, entertainment, sports commentator or sports in general, gambling, teaching—any career that involves travel or risk taking—are good choices for the Number 5.

Number 6 Birth Path

This is the number of compassion and responsibility. These children are very sensitive. Often intuitive, they need constant reassurance. They are naturally generous and want to be liked so much that they can give without thinking about how it will eventually affect them. These children can sacrifice their own needs for others, often thinking of themselves as the saviors of the family. They do not like hostility or physical or mental pain and will do everything they can to bring harmony by balancing negative or hostile forces. They are natural counselors; friends will come to them for advice. But the Number 6 needs to find the balance between being helpful and interfering. They must be cautious to not take on the lessons of others. Criticism can destroy them as they are often very critical of themselves. Consequently, it is important to help them have self-confidence and self-love. Because they have such a need to please, if they are encouraged, they will do well in school. But, if this child is abused or treated with disapproval, the child will stop trying. If ostracized by other students, they can become depressed and self-effacing. A word of warning: occasionally there are suicidal tendencies. Punishing these sensitive children is rarely necessary because they really don't want to hurt anyone. When it is necessary, the punishment should be administered lovingly, while continually telling the child they are not bad but it is the behavior that is not acceptable. Give the reasoning that explains the unacceptability of the behavior.

Because they are often very hard on themselves and hold onto shame and guilt forever, you must work to help them gain a healthy ego.

When the 6 is the Birth Day these children need balance and loving relationships. Encouragement will bring out the best in them, while criticism will cause withdrawal and a tendency toward martyrdom. Because they often hold onto shame and disapproval, if they clearly understand what is expected of them, and if they are given extensive love and emotional stroking and compliments, they will strive on their own not to do anything that would get them punished. However, as they grow into the teen years, their need for acceptance can cause them to follow the crowd. Thus, depending on their peer group can cause them to begin to act out in ways that could get them in trouble. The way to avoid this is to have a close relationship with your child so that they can come to you to discuss anything before they become involved in any negative behaviors. To receive trust from them, you must give trust in return.

Because they are quite empathic, do not lie to them. If something is wrong, talk with them. If you lie, they will think that they have disappointed you and will be extremely depressed.

Treating them with trust and love will get trust and love back. Criticism or lies will cause the negative behavior you are trying to avoid.

When the 6 appears in the Destiny Number, compassion, nurturing, honesty, responsibility, and trustworthiness is added to the other numbers.

Possible career choices for the Number 6: The six is the nurturing number so any job requiring caretaking can work for them, such as nursing, counseling, day care provider, hospice employee, doctor, or civil liberties attorney. Talented in expressing their feelings, they can excel as writers, musicians, actors, and clergy members. Family is important to them so anything that enhances families like adoption, cooking, or home interiors, may also work for the 6.

Number 7 Birth Path

Sevens are "unicorns." They are magical,

spiritual, unique individuals. Often misunderstood because of their immense intellect, they will appear to be like Spock from Star Trek: detached and analytical. However, they are actually very caring if you can get past their prickly exterior. They rapidly learn new information, but they can also bore easily, making school more drudgery than fun. If this happens, they can spend their time living in a world of their creation, finding it hard to live in the one that's real. The Number 7 Birth Path child needs to be in accelerated learning programs early-on and their parents must work with them at home as well. If encouraged to learn, and with understanding teachers, these people make wonderful scientists and inventors. Answering the greater questions of life is one of their major pursuits as they are natural problem solvers and would rather use their intellect than their emotions. Because they process the world as a whole, instead of like most of us—in pieces— they need alone time to process and sort all the information they absorb. The outdoors is a wonderful, nurturing place for them; hiking and fishing are good solitary pastimes. Sometimes their need for solitude and their unique way of learning can cause them to be diagnosed as on the autism spectrum. They are unique thinkers and are not necessarily people persons, disliking gossip and small talk and preferring to deal with deep thoughts and discussion instead. They may have few friends, but are extremely giving people and are easily used by others if they let them in. As money is not a motivator, they will need to be taught early the value of money and how to use it wisely. Because they can be very logical, unless they are mistreated, they will usually comply with punishment if the rules and consequences of defying the rules are clearly explained. If, however, the child has been allowed to become stubborn and opinionated, they will not listen and often repeat their negative behavior.

When 7 is the Birth Day, with their highly developed mind, intense curiosity, and desire to investigate the world, they can seem withdrawn, happy to spend hours alone on a computer, for example. The Number 7 Birth Day child may appear cold and aloof, sarcastic and unemotional. In short, the can appear to be the outsider.

When 7 is the Destiny Number their analytical mind and search for truth can add brilliance to any number. Unless the Number 7 Destiny is offset by more extroverted numbers like 1, 3, 5, or 8, this number will help create a more withdrawn personality.

Possible career choices for the Number 7: Number 7 persons are basically introverts, spiritual, serious, and restless hard workers. They have great powers of observation, thinking, and analyzing This is the searcher and seeker of truth. Children with a Number 7 Birth Path can make excellent researchers in any branch of science. They are well-suited to be innovators, spies, detectives, work with computers, become religious leaders, inventors, hypnotherapists, or metaphysicians. However, any pursuit that bores them will cause them to leave or, as often happens, do multiple jobs at once. Unfortunately, their need for solitude can cause them to withdraw. For that reason, this number has historically been considered the "number of the monk."

Number 8 Birth Path

The number 8 is a natural leader and has the capacity to accumulate wealth. They have talents in management and have the vision to reach long-range goals. With an ability to inspire people, they must learn to use their power to help others. Success, money, and popularity are great motivators for them. Consequently, these children can be quite competitive. Even though this number brings strong potential for success, that success is often won through experiencing many ups and downs. But an 8 has courage and determination and will usually rise to the top. Sports are a good outlet for them, but they must learn that they can't always be the star. Because these children are often competitive, it is important that their friends also be ambitious. The Number 8 child's behavior will mirror that of their friends. The child will be the best at whatever that child sees in life, even if it is being the best loser. They often seem old for their age as they want to express their opinions regarding everything that concerns them. So when punishment is needed, have them help decide on the punishment. But because they love to ague, make sure you and your child both clearly understand the terms and length of the punishment. Parents must guard against these children becoming self-important, arrogant, domineering, and feeling that their way is the only way. If their need for power becomes overblown, these children can be bullies and even argue with their teachers and parents or anyone in authority. They can also become stubborn, intolerant, and impatient. Being a tyrannical parent will only bring out the worst in this child. Never use the words, *because I said so*, unless you have explained the why of the situation first.

When 8 is the Birth Day it brings efficiency, power, ambition, leadership, self-confidence, and sound judgement. This is a wonderful number for people in business, but not necessarily for partnerships.

When 8 is the Destiny Number it adds the ability to achieve goals and lead. Highly competitive, it becomes very important to succeed and have power.

Possible career choices for the number 8: This number is gifted with natural leadership and the capacity to accumulate great wealth. Children with the Number 8 Birth Path will often become business leaders, doctors, financiers, generals, politicians, estate or business lawyers, real estate developers, publishers, and upper management workers.

Number 9 Birth Path

These children are kind humanitarians, deeply

concerned about the state of the world. Their deep compassion can cause them to be overly sensitive to anything negative and they will often feel guilty about things they could not possibly have caused or prevented. Because of this sensitivity, these children need to live in a mellow, balanced, loving environment. Cruelty, even outside their immediate families, such as within their culture and the world, can deeply affect these children. They are imaginative and creative; our current world rarely lives up to their desires. They can become fighters for world improvement. Sacrifice can become a strong part of their personality. If they do not have something to believe in, they can find happiness hard to come by, becoming moody and withdrawn, even potentially becoming addiction prone. If they become really depressed, the Number 9 Birth Path has the negative potential to become self-abusive or suicidal. They will do well in school, especially if they get loving rewards and praise for their hard work. If the environment is too competitive, the child might withdraw.

The 9 will always attempt to be helpers of the downtrodden; that can cause others to bully them. Punishment will be rarely necessary as long as these children have a secure, loving environment where the rules are explained and praise is given for good behavior instead of punishment for bad. These children can be so hard on themselves that punishment can often create more harm than good. They must learn the value of letting go of people, beliefs, and things when they no longer are relevant to their growth. It is imperative that these children develop a healthy self-image.

When the number 9 is the Birth Day it can help create broadminded, sensitive, creative, spiritual, idealistic, and compassionate children.

When the number 9 is the Destiny Number it adds the potential for a humanitarian nature. It is likely these children will want to be involved with causes or people who are trying to make a better world. There will be a visionary quality present.

This is a lifetime that is about completing a major stage in development. It can create geniuses and gurus.

Possible career choices for the Number 9: Children with a Number 9 Birth Path will often be attracted to the clergy, environmentalism, philanthropy, and counseling—any helping profession. They may desire to become activists or lobbyists. It is important for nines to leave a positive impact on the world.

Looking at Your Child's Heart's Desire Number

As stated before, the Heart's Desire Number indicates the inner motivations and deepest desires. If a child has a 1 Heart's desire, they crave independence. While a 2 craves partnerships and cooperation, a 3 desires creativity and peace. A 4 wants structure and security, while a 5 needs the freedom to have varied experiences. Then there are the 6s who need responsibility and closeness, while the 7 is in need of ideas and getting to the bottom of the deep, often hidden, aspects of life. The 8 needs healthy competition and recognition of his or her leadership abilities. The 9 desires to help the world become the spiritual, loving place it should be.

What happens if the Heart's Desire Number conflicts with the Birth Path Number? If this situation arises, there may be hidden conflict and lessons the Soul wants the "ego" (the child) to learn. If these children are worked with from an early age, this conflict can be somewhat mitigated. For instance, if the child's Birth Path is a 2, but the Heart's Desire is a 1, the child must be taught to work well with others and that if he truly is a leader, he or she will rise to the top anyway.

The **Personality** Number has much more to do with how the child will be seen by others than who they really are, and therefore, carries little weight in how to raise the child.

CHAPTER 7

If Your Child Has A Master Number

Make sure to determine if you find Master Numbers in your numerological calculation. As previously explained, if you arrive at any of the following four numbers in your calculation: 11, 22, 33, or 44, you do not reduce these numbers to a single digit. These four numbers are considered "Master Numbers" and indicate a decision by the Soul to present the child opportunities for exceptional experiences and growth. In general, it is thought that those with Master Numbers are naturally more intuitive and intelligent.

Number 11 Birth Path are children with a potential to be a source of inspiration and illumination for others. As children, they will not be well understood which can cause them to withdraw. They are often highly intuitive. This intuition can cause them to have insight without consciously knowing how. They can be quite introspective but can become too self-critical and begin to feel out of place. They are here to play a specific roll in this life but they must develop themselves sufficiently to be able to take advantage of the opportunities that lead them toward their goal. These children seem to develop slowly and can appear both confused and without direction. This is partially due to their extremely high expectations of themselves. They are very sensitive to stress and need a comfortable, low-key environment until they understand and appreciate their great powers and abilities. These people need to be diplomats, ambassadors, arbitrators, and humanitarians.

Number 22 Birth Path people are born under a very powerful number for success. This is the Master Builder Number—a person that can conceive in their mind of something big and create that thing in real life. However, their power is delicate as it exists in ideas and visions and must be actualized by bringing others into this dream. They must learn to integrate seemingly conflicting characteristics—their inspirations and their practical natures—in order to accomplish their life mission. They can unite a variety of differing people together to accomplish miracles. They will be ambitious which will help drive them toward their goals. They must understand that they need to share their vision but let others contribute, too. But because they can be so exacting, the Number 22 Birth Path child often lacks faith in the abilities of others. They can be overly controlling and even manipulative. Learning to be flexible instead of rigid will help them greatly. As adults, building lasting world

structures will be where they succeed, whether those structures are infrastructure, financial, government, law, or societal.

Number 33 Birth Path children are very sensitive, intuitive, and caring. They are the counselors, healers, and advisors of the world. They appear to be wise beyond their years, taking on responsibilities that are often difficult. Their world is the stage that they must work their magic on, helping humanity in both big and small ways. Concerned about anything or anyone that is downtrodden, these children will be rescuers. However, because of their immense sensitivity, they can have physical problems. These problems will often be thought of as psychosomatic nature, but in fact they are likely due to the child's ability to feel the pain of others so completely. They must guard against becoming depressed by the problems that surround them and feeling like failures when they cannot make everyone happy. Martyrdom is a

distinct possibility as they put the needs of others first at all times, then resent the fact that they are not being appreciated. Within the family, they will try to solve everyone's problems; they may attempt to be peacemakers to the point of meddling. A child with this number thrives when helping others. Consequently, working with large nonprofit institutions, teaching, writing, nursing and doctoring, social work, law, and government might be good career choices.

Number 44 Birth Path create children that are born wise. They have an inherent understanding of how to get things done, strive to get their own way, and often lead others. They are strong and seem to understand things that are much more advanced than you would expect someone their age to know. They like money and prestige and will work hard to get what they want. They are competitive, but often just convince others that their way is the best way. Their natural charisma draws people to them and

they make friends easily. Their need to control most situations indicates these children will need to understand the rules and consequences for breaking those rules, then they will argue about the rules until the punishment is completed or the adult gives up and does not enforce the punishment.

The Number 44 Birth Path tends to be quite trustworthy and will work to succeed at most tasks put before them. These children are here to be leaders and are meant to rise prominently in whatever endeavor they pursue. Working in leadership capacities they will do well in the military, government, medicine, large financial institutions, and heads of multi-national corporations.

CHAPTER 8

Karmic Challenge Numbers

Karmic challenge numbers are those numbers that are lacking in the child's name and that do not occur in the Birth Path, Expression, Day, or Heart's Desire numbers. As you now know, each letter has a corresponding number, and if a letter is absent from a name, so might be the corresponding number. For instance if the child's name was Thomas Joseph Smith, the number he would be lacking would be the number three as none of the 3 letters, C L or U, are present in his name. Consequently, the number 3 would be considered a karmic challenge number.

The karmic challenge numbers often indicate

missing traits, characteristics, or some important lesson that was not learned or handled well in a prior lifetime. (Inherent in the concept of karma is the understanding that the Soul creates many lifetimes. Think of a particular life time as a thread in the tapestry that is the Soul and that our experiences from all these threads can create habits, fears, relationship challenges, for example, that can come with us into different life threads.) These lessons can also indicate an important habit the child needs to cultivate in order to lead a more balanced life. It is important to note these deficiencies so that you can help the child develop in this particular area.

If your child is missing the number 1, they will find it difficult to express themselves and establish their individuality. Work with them on becoming self-starters and finding their own particular niche.

If the child is missing the number 2, you may notice a lack of sensitivity and intuition. The child may be impatient and have problems with punctuality. They will need to learn balance. Work with them to understand the feelings of others and to follow their gut instincts.

If the child is missing the number 3, they will suffer from a lack of self-confidence and could be quite shy. Their self-effacing attitude could also lead to an inability to make decisions. Help this child discover creative outlets that build their confidence. Never criticize them.

If the child is missing the number 4, these children may lack organizational skills. They find it hard to keep on task and complete projects because they are often scattered. They may also lack motivation. Teach them step-by-step processes for setting and meeting goals.

If the child is missing the number 5, they may lack drive, versatility, and the ability to multi-task. Consequently, they may require external pressure or motivation to accomplish anything. Teach them to value freedom and adventure. Work with them on tasks in such a way that they are exposed to many different ways to accomplish them.

If the child is missing the number 6, thinking of others first will not be natural for this child. They may have problems relating to others and find it very difficult to share feelings with anyone. These children need to be exposed to sharing and caring for a pet early. Teach them about empathy by showing them how their behaviors may feel to others and encourage them to express what they feel by listening to them without judgement.

If the child is missing the number 7, this child may be so immersed in his own world that he becomes completely insensitive and uncaring of anyone else. They can detach and remain aloof, but also be incapable of living independently. They must learn to relate to others and share their feelings and ideas openly. This can be done be honoring and welcoming conversation and discussions into your home and not discounting anyone's ideas.

If the child is missing the number 8, they may be impractical and bad at handling their finances. Lacking drive, they may abandon tasks when they are barely half done. They may also be impulsive and careless. They can be so naïve about money that they are frequently duped by others. They must learn to live in the real world within boundaries and think before they act. It may be a good idea to teach money skills early by establishing a savings account and paying them for completing assigned tasks.

If the child is missing the number 9, they may be insensitive and often overlook the needs of others. They can detach themselves from others and chose to live their way in their own world. You must work with them to be honest, candid, and more humanitarian. Get them involved with giving early and doing volunteer work where the pay off is not in money but in understanding and living for the greater good.

CHAPTER 9

Putting It All Together

One of the best ways to learn numerology is to put together the charts for many people, especially family members. This lets you use your own personal knowledge as a means to compare what the numbers indicate as well as give you additional insight into the person. Looking at the numerology of famous people can also provide a good learning experience. Let's take a look at a variety of people who share a common trait: a lifetime of living in the lime-light.

Number 1:

Actress and Singer Miley Ray Cyrus
Date of Birth: 11-23-1992

In determining Miley's Birth Path Number, we add together all the numbers of her birth date until a single digit is found:

$1 + 1 + 2 + 3 + 1 + 9 + 9 + 2 = 28$
reduces to 10 reduces to **1** Birth Path Number.

As we saw in the chapter on the Number 1 Birth Path, this is the number of the leader. The 1 creates independent individualists which Ms. Cyrus certainly has become. Now let's examine her other numbers to see how they might help or hinder her Birth Path Number.

Her full birth name, Miley Ray Cyrus, computes to a 68/14/5 Destiny Number, a 25/7 Heart's Desire Number and a 43/7 Personality Number. As you can see, there are a lot of 5s in her numbers. The energy of the number 5 adds flair, creativity, spontaneity, and free spiritedness to the 1 independence. However, until the person is old enough to master their potential, an overabundance of a number can also increase that number's negative qualities. The number only indicates potentialities not definite outcomes. In general, possible negative aspects of the number 5 include: sensualist, irresponsibility, sociopathic, and manipulative tendencies.

Other famous 1 Birth Paths: Tiger Woods, Steve Jobs, George Lucas, and Sting

Number 2:

Entertainment Mogul Madonna Louise Ciccone
Date of Birth: 8-16-1958

We compute Madonna's Birth Path as follows:
$8 + 1 + 6 + 1 + 9 + 5 + 8 = 38$
reduces to 11 reduces to **2** Birth Path Number.

When Madonna was just five years old, her mother died of breast cancer. Despite her young age, she had noticed changes in her mother's behavior, but she did not understand what was happening. Often "11/2 children" are quite intuitive and understand concepts without knowing how.

As stated earlier, the 11/2 can be quite introspective but can also become too self-critical and begin to feel out of place. In an interview conducted by *Vanity Fair*, Madonna revealed that she saw herself in her youth as a ". . .lonely girl who was searching for something. I cared about being good at something. I didn't shave my underarms and I didn't wear make-up like normal girls do. But I studied and I got good grades. . . I wanted to be somebody."

As is typical of many 11/2s, Madonna developed slowly, and at first was confused and without direction. This is partially due to her extremely high expectations of herself which certainly helped catapult her to later success. Additionally, Madonna's 8 Destiny Number added an ability to achieve goals and lead. As a highly competitive person, it became very important for her to attain success and have power. From the beginning, she ran her career like a business and continues to be successful.

Other famous 2 Birth Paths: Presidents Barack Obama and Bill Clinton, Vice-President Al Gore, Jennifer Aniston, and Tim McGraw.

Number 3:

**Academy Award Winning Actress Alicia Christian (Jodie) Foster
Date of Birth: 11-19-1962**

Jodie Foster's Birth Path computation:

$1 + 1 + 1 + 9 + 1 + 9 + 6 + 2 = 30$
reduces to **3** Birth Path Number.

People with 3s in their numerology are often feminine, attractive, gentle children. Jodie Foster started her career at age three as a child model and two years later began acting in the television show *Mayberry RFD*. The number 3 often produces creative, optimistic, communicative, imaginative, and sociable children. Not surprisingly, acting and modeling can be enticing careers.

With a 3 Destiny Number as well, Jodie Foster

is one of the few child actors that have continued their success into adulthood. Additionally, with her 1 Birth Day adding independence and leadership, she not surprisingly, expanded her creative skills by becoming a producer and director. Foster has a 5 Heart's Desire which adds a layer of risk-taking and adventure to her personality.

Other famous 3 Birth Paths include: Hillary Clinton, Alan Alda, Barbara Walters, Snoop Dog, Linda McCartney, and John Travolta.

Number 4:

Media Mogul Oprah Gail Winfrey
Date of Birth: 1-29-1954

Oprah Winfrey's Birth Path computation:

$1 + 2 + 9 + 1 + 9 + 5 + 4 = 31$
which reduces to a **4** Birth Path Number.

A person with the number 4 is likely to have traits of being steadfast, practical, organized, pragmatic, trustworthy, and determined; they are capable of producing anything through hard work. The Number 4 also relates to high morals, traditional values, honesty and integrity, inner-wisdom, security, self-control, loyalty, conscientiousness, reality and realistic values, stability and dignity.

Winfrey was born into poverty in rural Mississippi to a teenage, single mother. She has stated she was molested during her childhood and early teens and became pregnant, but that her baby died. After moving in with the man she calls her father, a barber in Tennessee, Winfrey landed a job in radio while still in high school and began co-anchoring the local evening news at the age of 19. Her emotional, ad-lib delivery eventually got her transferred to the daytime-talk-show arena, and after boosting a third-rated local Chicago talk show to first place, she launched her own production company and became internationally syndicated. She raised herself out of poverty and a desperate childhood as a result of her perseverance, determination, and hard work, eventually becoming one of the most successful women in the world.

Oprah's Birth Path Number 4 is enhanced by her Heart's Desire 4. This accentuated her deep desire for security and stability in her life. With an 11/2 Master Number Birth Day, Winfrey was fated to make her mark in the world. People with this number possess the potential to be a source of inspiration and illumination for others. Additionally, Winfrey has a 7 Destiny Number which can charge her Birth Path with brilliance, spirituality, intuition, and the ability to analyze and reason.

Other famous 4 Birth paths include: Arnold Schwarzenegger, Bono, Bill Gates, Elton John, and Jewell.

Number 5:

Performer Michael Phillip (Mick) Jagger
Date of Birth: 7-26-1943

Rolling Stones front man Mick Jagger's Birth

Path computation is:

$$7 + 2 + 6 + 1 + 9 + 4 + 3 = 23$$
which reduces to a **5** Birth Path Number.

Having the number 5 Birth Path adds flare, excitement, adventure, and the need for many and varied experiences. This is the person that must try everything at least once. No matter how wild these people are, no matter how many vices they may have, they usually come through their lives easily with very few ill effects. People like them and they love to be the center of attention.

However, with the 8 Birth Path it is likely that Jagger needs to feel that he's in control of his life and his vocation. His career as the front man for the Rolling Stones is a good choice for him.

Jagger's numbers indicate he likes ease and is very creative: the Heart's Desire 3. And his Destiny 1 adds to his need to be a leader, independent, and unique.

Other famous 5 Birth Paths include: Steven Spielberg, Liv Tyler, Willie Nelson, Don Johnson, and Ron Howard.

Number 6:

Singer Billie Eilish Pirate Baird O'Connell
Date of Birth: 12-18-2001

1 + 2 + 1 + 8 + 2 + 0 + 0 + 1 = 15
which reduces to a 6 Birth Path.

Six is the number that indicates potentials for family responsibility, nurturer, martyr, the champion of the downtrodden, intellectual creativity, discrimination, imagination, perfection, and the ability to use the imagination and the intellect in combination.

Billie Eilish is a singer, songwriter who exploded onto the music scene in 2015 with the song "Ocean Eyes" which was written by her brother. After just two weeks on the music platform Sound Cloud, it had been listened to several hundred thousand times. The next year, she signed her first recording contract with Apple records.

Eilish grew up in a close-knit family of actors and musicians and was homeschooled. Even with her profound success, she still lives with her family. An activist, she has fought for animal rights, veganism, and voting rights by working to register voters. She has talked publicly about her mental health challenges that began after an injury forced her quit dancing when she was 13. She found herself depressed, anxious, and suffered from body image issues that led her to become a cutter.

As a 6 Birth Path, she craves love and is very sensitive, especially to criticism. Family is very important to the 6 and having a supportive family has helped Eilish overcome much of her depressive disorder.

She is known to be a bit reclusive and to value her alone time. This is due to having both a 7 Hearts Desire and Destiny number.

Other famous 6 Birth Paths include: Albert Einstein, Eddy Murphy, Goldie Hawn, Jennifer Lawrence, and George W. Bush.

Number 7:

Actor John (Johnny) Christopher Depp II
Date of Birth: 6-9-1963

$6 + 9 + 1 + 9 + 6 + 3 = 34$
which reduces to a 7 Birth Path

As a 7 Birth Path, Depp has numbers indicating tendencies to be the seeker, the thinker, the searcher of truth. The 7 doesn't take anything at face value—it is always trying to understand the underlying, hidden truths.

Sevens have an air of mystery and do not want others to know who they are. Intellectual, analytical, intuitive, reserved, a natural inclination toward spiritual subjects, aloof, loner, pessimistic, secretive, and insecure—these are some of the qualities of those born into the 7th Birth Path.

With a brilliant but unique mind, 7s often feel uncomfortable with school and Depp quit high school at age 15. Because of his need to grow and learn, he chose to experience as much of life as soon as possible and is quoted as saying, "I started smoking at 12, lost my virginity at 13, and did every kind of drug there was by 14. Pretty much any drug you can name, I've done it. I wouldn't say I was bad or malicious, I was just curious."

People with a 7 Birth Path are idealists that wish to live in an idealized world. They are often drawn to the outcasts of the world, often feeling they are outcasts themselves.

Because 7s can be loners or introverts, they are most comfortable by themselves. They can happily give up the stress and turmoil of a busy life in favor of a quiet, peaceful life of solitude. They value their independence and can find it difficult to relate to others especially in close personal relationships. Depp has been involved and married to several different women, but none have lasted long. With his 11/2 Destiny, Depp would desire closeness, even though it is hard to come by due to his natural solitary nature.

Other famous 7 Birth Paths include: George Bush Sr., Dr. Phil McGraw, Princess Diana, Mel Gibson, and Julia Roberts.

Number 8:

Academy Award Winning Actress Elizabeth Rosemond Taylor
Date of Birth: 2-27-1932

2 + 2 + 7 + 1 + 9 + 3 + 2 = 26
which reduces to an 8 Birth Path.

The 8 Birth Path is known for qualities that include strength as a leader as well as the capacity to accumulate great wealth despite ups and downs. They can inspire people. They can achieve powerful positions while also being stubborn, arrogant, and domineering. Arguably, Taylor's life included many of these traits.

Elizabeth Taylor began her acting career at the age of nine. By the time she was 12, her breakout role in the movie *National Velvet* made her one of the world's most popular teen stars. People with the number 8 Birth Path like control over their own lives, so it fits that despite being one of MGM's most bankable stars, Taylor wished to end her career when she was in her twenties. She resented the studio's control over her and disliked many of the films she was being assigned. Yet she continued to act, becoming the first actress to earn $1,000,000 for a movie role. She is considered one of the last major stars to have come out of the old Hollywood studio system.

In 2006, Taylor introduced a line of diamond and precious stone jewelry called "House of Taylor." The designs are said to be inspired by favorite pieces in her own collection. She actually wrote a book on jewelry and was considered to be an authority on the subject.

In an era where women's roles were very traditional, Taylor took on roles that represented powerful women not content to live lives orchestrated for them. She has been labeled by some as one of modern society's first feminists.

Her stormy love life is well known. She was married eight times, twice to her "Soul Mate" Richard Burton.

Taylor has a 9 Day Number. Traits often seen in this context include sensitivity, creativity, spiritual emphasis, idealism, and compassion. These different facets would certainly have helped her to play a variety of roles as an actress. Arguably, her most significant contribution—her desire to dedicate her life to helping AIDS-related charities and fundraisers—is consistent with the 9 Day Number working in cooperation with the 8 Birth Path. Her commitment to public service was significant. In addition to helping co-found the American Foundation for AIDS Research, Taylor formed her own foundation, the Elizabeth Taylor Aids Foundation with the purpose of providing direct services for people living with AIDS around the world.

With a 3 Destiny Number, Taylor perfectly imbued the qualities of the 3 Destiny; she was known for her beauty, creativity, and sensitivity. These qualities helped her to uplift and empower others.

Other famous 8 Birth Path include: Joni Mitchell, Richard Gere, Barbara Streisand, Victor Frankl, Faith Hill, and Stevie Nicks.

Number 9:

Singer and actress Whitney Elizabeth Houston
Date of Birth: 8–9–1963

$8 + 9 + 1 + 9 + 6 + 3 = 36$
which reduces to a **9** Birth Path.

The number 9 Birth Path produces kind humanitarians, deeply concerned about the state of the world. Their compassion can cause them to be overly sensitive to anything negative and they will often feel guilty about things they could not possibly have caused or prevented. Because of this sensitivity, they need to live in a mellow, balanced, loving environment. Events even outside their immediate families, such as within their culture and the world, can deeply affect them.

Houston came from a middle class family filled with entertainers. Her mother was a backup singer for Elvis Presley. Singers Dionne Warwick and Dee Dee Warwick were her first cousins. At the age of 11, Houston began performing as a soloist in her church's junior gospel choir. At age 15, Houston sang background vocals for Chaka Khan and Lou Rawls. In the early 80s, Houston started working as a fashion model after a photographer saw her at Carnegie Hall singing with her mother. She appeared in *Seventeen Magazine*, one of the first women of color on the cover of the magazine. She was also featured in layouts in the pages of *Glamour*, *Cosmopolitan*, and *Young Miss*. Her looks and girl-next-door charm made her one of the most sought after teen models of that time.

Houston's debut album *Whitney Houston* was released in February of 1985. *Rolling Stone* magazine praised Houston, calling her "one of the most exciting new voices in years," while the *New York Times* called the album "an impressive, musically conservative showcase for an exceptional vocal talent." Her career soared and she even tried her hand at acting, staring with Kevin Costner in *The Body Guard*.

Despite her outward success, it is now evident how challenging Houston's personal life was. This is not uncommon for 9s; they often have difficult lives. Houston's situation was compounded by the fact she also had a 9 Birth Day. Her difficulties appeared to begin after her marriage to Bobby Brown in 1992. There were rumors of drug and physical abuse. Sadly, these are common problems for the very sensitive 9.

Additionally, Houston's 6 Destiny increased her sensitivity. It also explains why she could not easily pull herself away Brown. The 6 in this position increased her desire to be in a marriage, making her even more susceptible to staying or going back to an abusive relationship.

Other famous 9 Birth paths include: Elvis Presley, Bob Marley, Harrison Ford, Robin Williams, and Jimi Hendrix.

Just for Fun Practice Charts

Joseph Robinette Biden
Birthdate: 11-20-1942

Day Number:

Birth Path Number:

Destiny/Expression Number:

Heart's Desire Number:

Personality Number:

Missing Numbers:

Just for Fun Practice Charts

Kamala Devi Harris
Birthdate: 10-20-1964

Day Number:

Birth Path Number:

Destiny/Expression Number:

Heart's Desire Number:

Personality Number:

Missing Numbers:

Just for Fun Practice Charts

**Donald John Trump
Birthdate: 6-14-1946**

Day Number:

Birth Path Number:

Destiny/Expression Number:

Heart's Desire Number:

Personality Number:

Missing Numbers:

Just for Fun Practice Charts

Taylor Alison Swift
Birthdate: 12-13-1989

Day Number:

Birth Path Number:

Destiny/Expression Number:

Heart's Desire Number:

Personality Number:

Missing Numbers:

Just for Fun Practice Charts

Belcalis Marlenis Almazar (Cardi B)
Birthdate: 10-11-1992

Day Number:

Birth Path Number:

Destiny/Expression Number:

Heart's Desire Number:

Personality Number:

Missing Numbers:

Just for Fun Practice Charts

Beyond Giselle Knowles
Birthdate: 9-4-1981

Day Number:

Birth Path Number:

Destiny/Expression Number:

Heart's Desire Number:

Personality Number:

Missing Numbers:

Just for Fun Practice Charts

NAME: _____

Day Number:

Birth Path Number:

Destiny/Expression Number:

Heart's Desire Number:

Personality Number:

Missing Numbers:

Just for Fun Practice Charts

NAME: _____

Day Number:

Birth Path Number:

Destiny/Expression Number:

Heart's Desire Number:

Personality Number:

Missing Numbers:

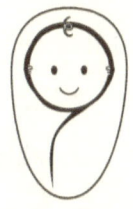

Conclusion

Raising your child well is arguably the single most difficult job anyone can undertake. That adorable baby that melts your heart is an extremely complex being. As every parent would agree, there is no one-size-fits-all when it comes to parenting. Any tool we can use to give us greater insight into the particular personality traits of these amazing little people is well worth studying.

The most important thing I hope you will get from this book is an understanding of the potential tendencies of your children. Compute the numerology of your children or grandchildren;

study the information about what the numbers mean while you are thinking about the child in your life. Just keep in mind that every child must be allowed to develop in his or her own natural way. If you hope to raise a star athlete (a Number 5 or 8), forcing your son who is a Number 3 Birth Path to be a football player might not work well. Of course an examination of all the numbers and how they relate to one another is the important thing. But, if you have a creative, less-competitive child, forcing them to become competitive will cause them harm. It's likely that encouraging the child's creativity will help the child to be happier and thus easier, or certainly more pleasant, to raise. It is my hope that the numerological information you obtain will give you helpful insight into what makes your precious child tick.

References

The Kabbalah recognizes the mystical significance of numbers. See: kabbalah.com.

For further reading on the subject of numerology see: Dr. Juno Jordan (1984) *Numerology, the Romance in Your Name.* DeVorss & Company.

Dan Millman, (1993) *The Life You Were Born to Live*, HJ Kramer.

Miley Cyrus is much more complex than her Hannah Montana image reflected. See: billboard.com/articles/columns/pop-shop/6575667/miley-cyrus-more-than-one-thing

A student of the Kabbalah, Madonna explains the impact of the death of her mother: vanityfair.com/news/2008/05/madonna200805

Identified as a "gifted child," Jodie Foster's successes are lengthy and diverse: biography.com/people/jodie-foster-9299556

Brilliant in many ways, Oprah Winfrey learned to read when she was only two-and-a-half, thanks to the guidance of her grandmother: notablebiographies.com/We-Z/Winfrey-Oprah.html

Never one to shy from the lime-light, Mick Jagger willingly answers interview questions: mickjagger.com/interviews/bbc-mick-jagger-answers-your-questions

An uplifting video, Billie Eilish engages in Carpool Karaoke with James Corden. Search: Youtube & Eilish & Carpool Karaoke.

Johnny Depp's life continues to throw him curve balls: theguardian.com/film/2020/nov/03/the-fall-of-johnny-depp-how-the-worlds-most-beautiful-movie-star-turned-very-ugly

Citation for Depp quote: imdb.com/name/nm0000136/bio?ref_=nm_ov_bio_sm

Elizabeth's Taylor's Aids Foundation continues to do the work to which she was so committed: elizabethtayloraidsfoundation.org/

Understandably devastated by her daughter's death, Whitney Houston's mother tries to understand what went wrong: huffingtonpost.com/2013/01/24/whitney-houston-mother-cissy-houston-could-i-have-saved-her_n_2542684.html

About the Author

Joan L. Scibienski has been a professional intuitive consultant, numerologist, and astrologer working with thousands of clients for over 40 years. She has lectured and taught classes on psychic development and spiritual topics throughout the U.S., Canada, and parts of Europe. She holds degrees in nursing, psychology, and metaphysics.

Joan is also the author of **The Ariana Series**: *Be the Light*, *Becoming the Light*, and *Fighting Darkness*. Through this series she is attempting to educate the public on psychic phenomenon, spirituality, and helping our beautiful planet to thrive.

Her workbook, *You Were Born Psychic: A Metaphysical Approach to Uncovering & Using Your Abilities*, is designed to unlock a person's natural abilities.

For more information about Joan's work:
www.intuitivedirections.com

Follow Joan on social media:
@thecircleledbyjoan

Learn about Joan's unique spiritual & metaphysical membership website:
www.thecirclegrp.com

www.ingramcontent.com/pod-product-compliance
Lightning Source LLC
Chambersburg PA
CBHW021427070526
44577CB00001B/99